ROBERT MANGOLD

ROBERT MANGOLD

RECENT PAINTINGS AND DRAWINGS

March 18 - April 23, 1994

THE PACE GALLERY 142 Greene Street, New York City
PACE DRAWINGS 32 East 57th Street, New York City

PaceWildenstein

THREE STATEMENTS ABOUT THE PAINTINGS OF ROBERT MANGOLD
By John Yau

I.

Ever since the late 1960's, when Robert Mangold first painted on canvas, as well as introduced dark drawing lines into his work, he has continued to discover and register revelations about the provisional relationships between seeing and knowing, between the unified whole and its individualized parts. At the same time, by introducing a kind of naked or undisguised drawing into his painting when he did, Mangold was one of the few abstract artists of his generation to go against the widely accepted critical proscriptions against drawing. Mangold's incorporation of drawing into painting went beyond being a rebellious reaction against critics and his Minimalist peers. Through his integration of drawing and shape, Mangold was able to transform both Minimalism's anti-metaphorical aesthetic and emphasis on facticity into an expansive possibility—one that encouraged the viewer's mental and visual engagement with the work of art.

Mangold's use of drawing enabled him to begin articulating an open-ended dialectic which was capable of acknowledging the inevitable pressures of doubt, the human need for metaphors, and the inescapable desire for images. In retrospect, it is clear that Mangold redefined abstract painting by introducing palpable instances of self-criticality into Minimalism, which valorized a pragmatic materialist approach, static objects and a timeless present. Through his seamless synthesis of drawing and painting, and the ways he enabled them to become self-critical mirrors of each other, Mangold was able to begin addressing a deeper and broader set of philosophical issues than the ones defined as historically necessary by his peers. Thus, if anything has become evident about Mangold's career, it is that over the past 25 years he has continually found ways to address the challenge that "painting is dead"—a declaration that has been, since the mid-1950's and the untimely death of Jackson Pollock, regularly repackaged by numerous critics and artists alike.

That Mangold has always remained steadfastly committed to painting, particularly to the dialectics of the provisional relationships of its basic elements (drawing and shape, color and surface) suggests that he has dedicated himself to a daunting task: the recovery of painting from the critical discourses that constantly threaten its vitality. And because he has set out to recover painting from the realm of stable discourse and fixed definitions, it should be evident that Robert Mangold has continued down the path that in America was first investigated by the Abstract Expressionists.

The deepest tradition of painting, the one that embodies renewal, is not simply a cycle of stylistic reactions and formal refinements that can be easily accounted for in language. Rather, the vitality of art is made evident in the unexpected yet meaningful disruptions that occur, and in which something basic is recovered. Thus Pollock recovers paint, the psychic resonance of its elemental state of liquidity, from the historical pressure to depict, while Mangold recovers line and image from the stabilized realm of reference and closure. And yet, what Pollock and Mangold have in common is their belief in drawing, not as a referential force, but as an elemental one. For them, drawing is a part of painting the way, for a poet, sounds are a necessary and inextricable part of a poem.

II.

In his first mature paintings, which were done in the mid-1960's, Mangold applied dry, matte color to cut sections of plywood. Either notched or the result of two irregular geometric sections being abutted together, these monochromatic works existed as much in the province of wall relief and architecture as in the place occupied by painting, and were seen as Minimalist works alongside Stella's shaped canvases and Ryman's white squares. In 1965, when these paintings were first shown, Mangold titled the exhibition "Walls and Areas," and thus connected himself to the fresco painting from the outset of his career. The difference was that Mangold's paintings were "walls" that could be easily moved from one place to another. As Klaus Kertess has so astutely pointed out: "His frescoes, like his culture, are nomadic (portable) and fragmentary." At the same time, Mangold's paintings are a combination of shape and surface, which sets his work apart from that of Frank Stella, who insisted that a painting was an inviolable object. In this regard, their early work can be said to foreshadow their current attitudes toward painting or, in the case of Stella, free-standing sculptural objects.

Starting in the late 1960's, during the Vietnam War and race riots in America, Mangold began to use drawing to raise not only explicit questions about the relationship between perception and knowledge, but also to offer an implicit criticism of the prevailing attitude in the art world, an attitude which Frank Stella effectively summed up when he stated "What you see is what you see." Stella's nonreflective aestheticizing of experience separates art from the world and is ultimately hierarchical in that it posits that art is superior to life. I suspect Mangold concluded that Stella's statement was too essentializing and ultimately wrong, and felt that both the world and art could never be that stable and simple.

In *Distorted Circle within a Polygon (Yellow-ochre)*, 1972, for example, the viewer sees an egg-like, graphite circle within a yellow-ochre polygon, and wonders whether the circle determined the painting's physical shape or vice versa. Mangold's non-hierarchical attitude toward drawing and painting challenges the notion that either the structure determines the composition or the use of repetitive composition determines the structure. In these and other paintings from the late 1960's and early 70's, it is clear that Mangold was unable to accept the models of deductive or additive logic associated with Minimalism, Color Field painting, and Pop art, and the belief that one thing necessarily followed another. In a larger sense, Mangold was, in effect, questioning the way critics and artists had reduced art history to a tale about progress, a tale which, in retrospect, seems out of sync with the times.

Mangold is one of the few artists who recognizes the stakes involved in Pollock's attempt to make art exist in the same physical world as the viewer. Pollock's poured paintings aren't simply a formal innovation on his part, the result of an aesthetic desire to rid art of such fictive possibilities as illusionism. Like many of his Abstract Expressionist peers, Pollock wanted to banish a deeper illusionism from art, the notion that art is a privileged moment which exists outside of time and change. Pollock's desire, as well as his achievement, are what have been misunderstood as well as misrepresented by the critics who have summarized the transition from Abstract Expressionism to Minimalism, Pop art, and Color Field painting. For while these critics are fierce proponents of all-over or nonhierarchical composition, they still stubbornly cling to the belief that the realm of aesthetic experience is superior to that of life.

However, rather than aestheticizing the viewer's experience by making a pure, self-contained statement, Mangold admits into his art the realization that the world is a constantly changing place. He achieves this by imaginatively utilizing a nonhierarchical vocabulary of destabilized elements. Thus, in his recent paintings, the double ellipse he has drawn is simultaneously a line and an image, as well as possibly a sign of some sort and a perspectival rendering. Equally open-ended is the shaped picture plane, which is both flat and seemingly spatial; and, while the plane is parallel to the wall, its shape evokes the possibility that it is somehow tilting and perhaps even twisting in and through space. Without fanfare or theatrics, Mangold manages to encourage these diverse modes of perception and reading without privileging any one of them.

What makes Mangold's art contiguous with our experience of the world is his ability to articulate a provisional unity which embodies constantly changing relationships among its elements. He has not only eschewed illusionism in both drawing and painting, but he has also rejected the illusion that art can embody a timeless, unchanging moment, that it can offer us a sanctuary from a changing world, as well as from time. Consequently, Mangold's paintings embody neither a timeless, self-contained wholeness nor continue the societal illusion that a pure aesthetic experience is possible, desirable and even superior to all other experience.

If abstraction is going to remain a vital force, that is to say something that transcends the realm of aesthetics, it is because an artist such as Robert Mangold has steadfastly found ways to make paintings that bridge the gap between the refined perceptions one associates with all art and the raw ones inherent in life. That he has done so without making reference to either personal feelings or specific events in the world should not be seen as an evasion, but as an attempt to make art that can be in and of the world without supporting society's commodification of each and every individual's self-expression and desire.

III.

In *Plane/Figure Series*, Mangold draws one looping line to articulate a double ellipse on a two-panel painting. The rounder, wider ellipse joins the narrower, sleeker ellipse at a right angle. This relational configuration evokes the possibility that the narrower one is a perspectival rendering of the wider one, a reading which the two panels neither fully underscore nor completely deny. At the same time, the line of the fatter one seems to move far more quickly once it begins to define the narrower one. In order to pace our reading of this double ellipse, and make each part of it equal, we are tempted to see the it as a nonreferential image in which one ellipse supports the other. In this regard, they become distinct entities. And yet, might it not be possible that each ellipse cordons off the same amount of area? Thus, while the double ellipse seems to be a single unit, every mode of reading we apply to it—whether as an inseparable entity made of distinct elements or as separate but joined elements—encounters doubt. Finally, it should be pointed out that Mangold achieves this state of ambiguity with a single drawn line, and that this line is something we read and analyze even as we see its austerely sensual, physical presence in the painting.

By making doubt and ambiguity an integral part of his paintings, Mangold acknowledges two recognitions. There are limits to human knowledge, and there is no one or essential way to comprehend the world. The relationship between the perceiving mind and the animal senses is continually shifting, a basic fact of human consciousness which Mangold constantly makes vivid. We live in a relentlessly changing world, and all our perceptions and conclusions are, at best, provisional. In this regard, Mangold is a secular, abstract artist who investigates the realm of consciousness without resorting to either emblems of faith or signs of transcendence. He has more in common philosophically with Wittgenstein than with any existentialist, ethical or religious thinker.

The doubts inherent to the act of seeing, which is an integral part of Mangold's use of drawing, is echoed by the physical shape of the two-panel painting. Each rectangle has one right angle comprised of an equally sized bottom and interior edge. The exterior sides, however, are slanted toward the center meridian, the physical line made by the two rectangles being abutted together. The combination of the interior vertical space (or line) made by the two rectangles, and the different lengths and angles of their exterior, inwardly slanting edges evoke the possibility that some force is pressing against or squeezing the sides of the entire painting. Working in counterpoint to the exterior pressure is the central meridian, and the right angle it forms with the painting's bottom edge.

The tension between exterior pressure and interior resoluteness is, in turn, echoed by the ellipses, which are imperfect circles. As the irregular rectangles make evident, a perfect circle could not fit cleanly into either of them or into the whole painting together. Finally, because the equally sized bottom edges parallel the floor, and the central meridian where the two rectangles meet is perfectly vertical, one is tempted to read the entire work, its slanting exterior and vertical interior edges (compositional lines), as a palpable metaphor of Mangold's views about the current state of painting, that painting continues to maintain its authority despite internal doubts and external pressures.

In this recent series, more than in any other, Mangold openly recognizes that an abstract painting is a contingent entity that must somehow maintain both its authority and dignity even though it is continually threatened by a host of external forces. And within his decisions about shape and composition one sees a steadfast but unassuming display of his belief in the act of painting. However, instead of calling our attention to his belief, Mangold locates it in a number of specific but untheatrical acts. In recognizing this integral feature of Mangold's paintings we might also wish to further consider whether the loudest believer (or disbeliever) is truly authentic or not.

In *Plane/Figure Series C (Double Panel)*, 1993, Mangold used a roller to paint both panels a dry, brownish-red. Like his other paintings, the color is specific but nonreferential, and seems as if it could be derived from both industry and nature, be both a manmade chemical and a natural substance, like the bark of a rotting tree. In that the color seems both impure (dirty?) and right, it also evokes a fresco exposed to the effects of time.

The right edge slants at a slightly more severe angle than the left edge, and the placement of the central meridian of the two rectangles is determined by virtue of the fact that in both panels the bottom edges are of equal lengths. The central dividing line is what unifies the painting, and holds it together. The sense that the entire shape of the painting is slowly and inexorably collapsing is underscored by the placement of the double ellipse.

The wider, rounder ellipse starts in the bottom left corner and rises at an angle toward the right-hand edge; the angle of its tilt is determined by both the width of the ellipse and the angle defined by the bottom and left edge. Echoing this is the sleeker, thinner ellipse, which rises from the narrower, right-hand corner and touches the right upper edge of the left panel.

Are the geometric shapes of the panels determined by the width of the ellipse? Or did the configuration of the double ellipse determine each panel's shape? Mangold's paintings are allover compositions, in that the viewer cannot deduce that any one element (drawing, shape, color) determined and thus preceded any other. We must see the whole painting, even as we begin engaging with both the changing relationship and identity of its elements.

For all their distinctiveness and individuality, each element of the painting exists in relationship to the rest of the parts, and helps define the whole. Stable and sturdy, the ellipses lean against each other like the boulders at Stonehenge, thus echoing the exterior edges of the two panels. The central meridian, its physically absent line, also evokes a stable but, in this case, divided world. Wholeness, the painting suggests, is made up of distinct and almost completely self-sufficient parts.

While the physical scale of the largest paintings in this series extends beyond breadth of human gesture, the equally large drawing within—its carefully calibrated looping line—is made by hand. Expressiveness is held in check, but not denied. The paintings exist in the same world we inhabit, and they resonate in the mind's eye long after we have stopped looking at them. Mangold has articulated a realm of contemplativeness in which further insights into human consciousness are disclosed. When a painting exists in the realm of contemplativeness rather than being simply another thing, a fancy bauble, in the visible world, the painter has given the viewer a gift. Robert Mangold is such a painter.

Plane/Figure Series A (Double Panel) Study, 1993
acrylic and black pencil on canvas, 56¼ x 84¼"

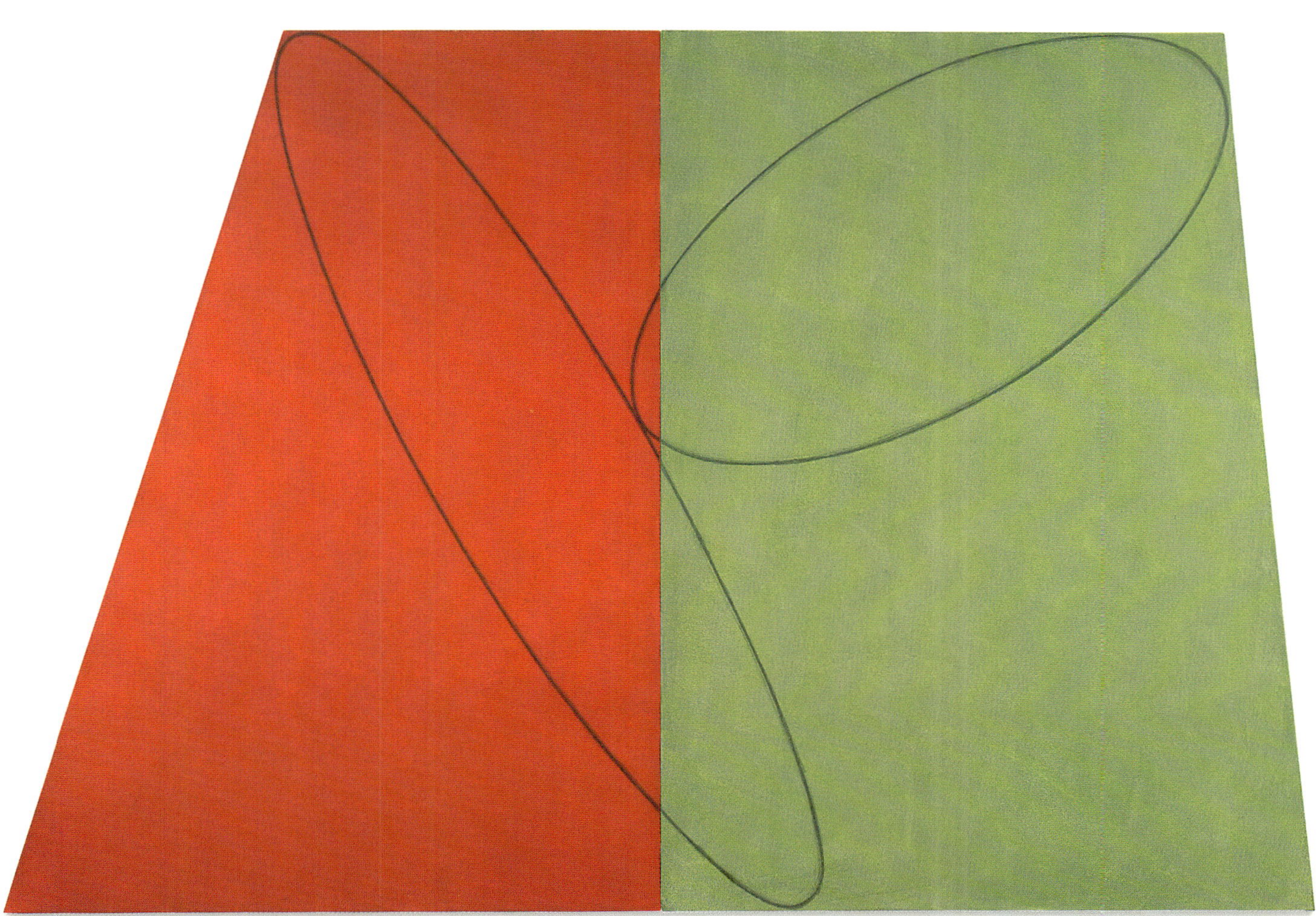

Plane/Figure Series B (Double Panel) Study, 1993
acrylic and black pencil on canvas, 56¼ x 84½"

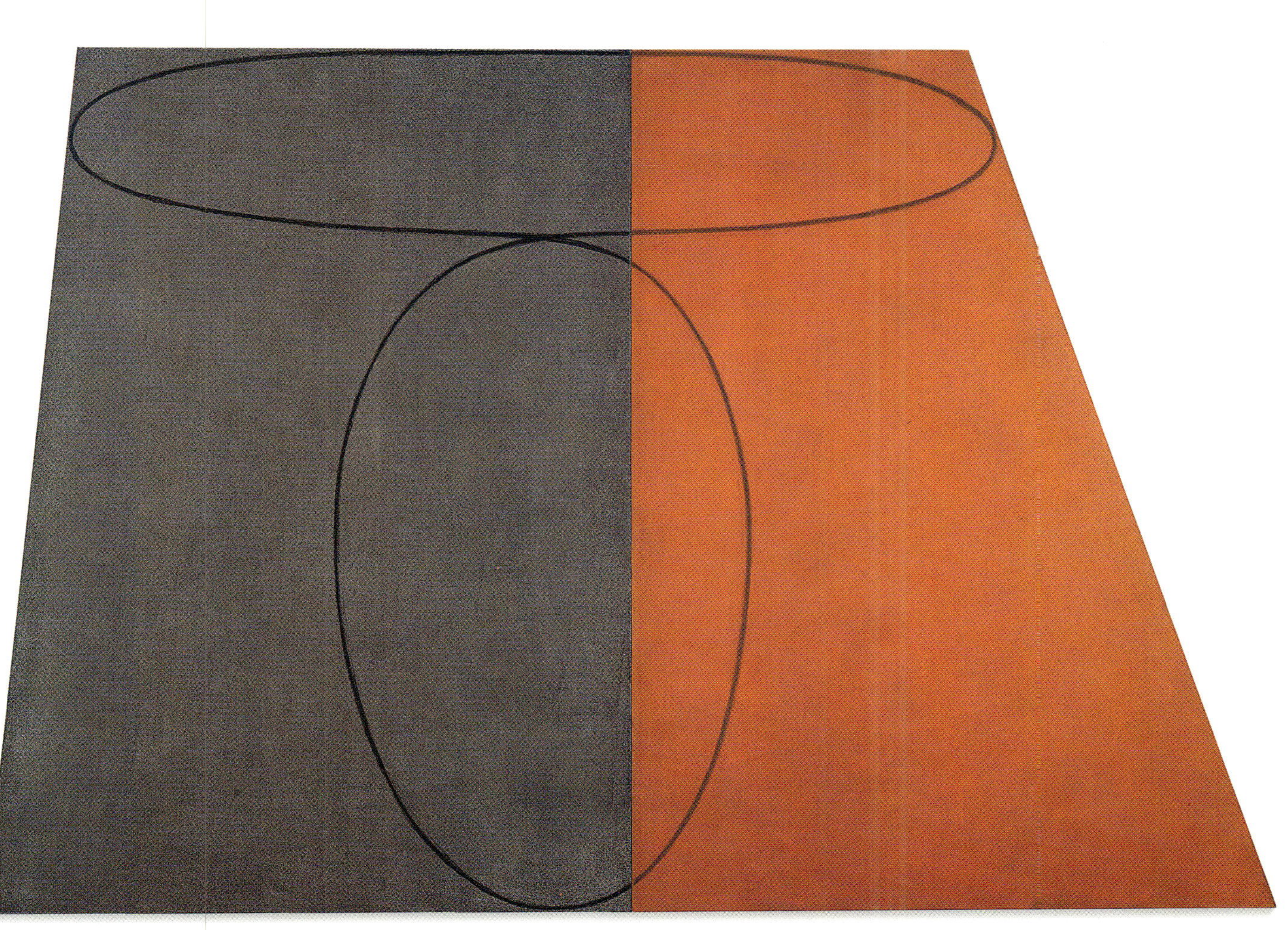

Plane/Figure Series B (Double Panel), 1993
acrylic and black pencil on canvas, 112 x 168"
Installation at Hallen für neue Kunst, Schaffhausen, Switzerland, 1993.

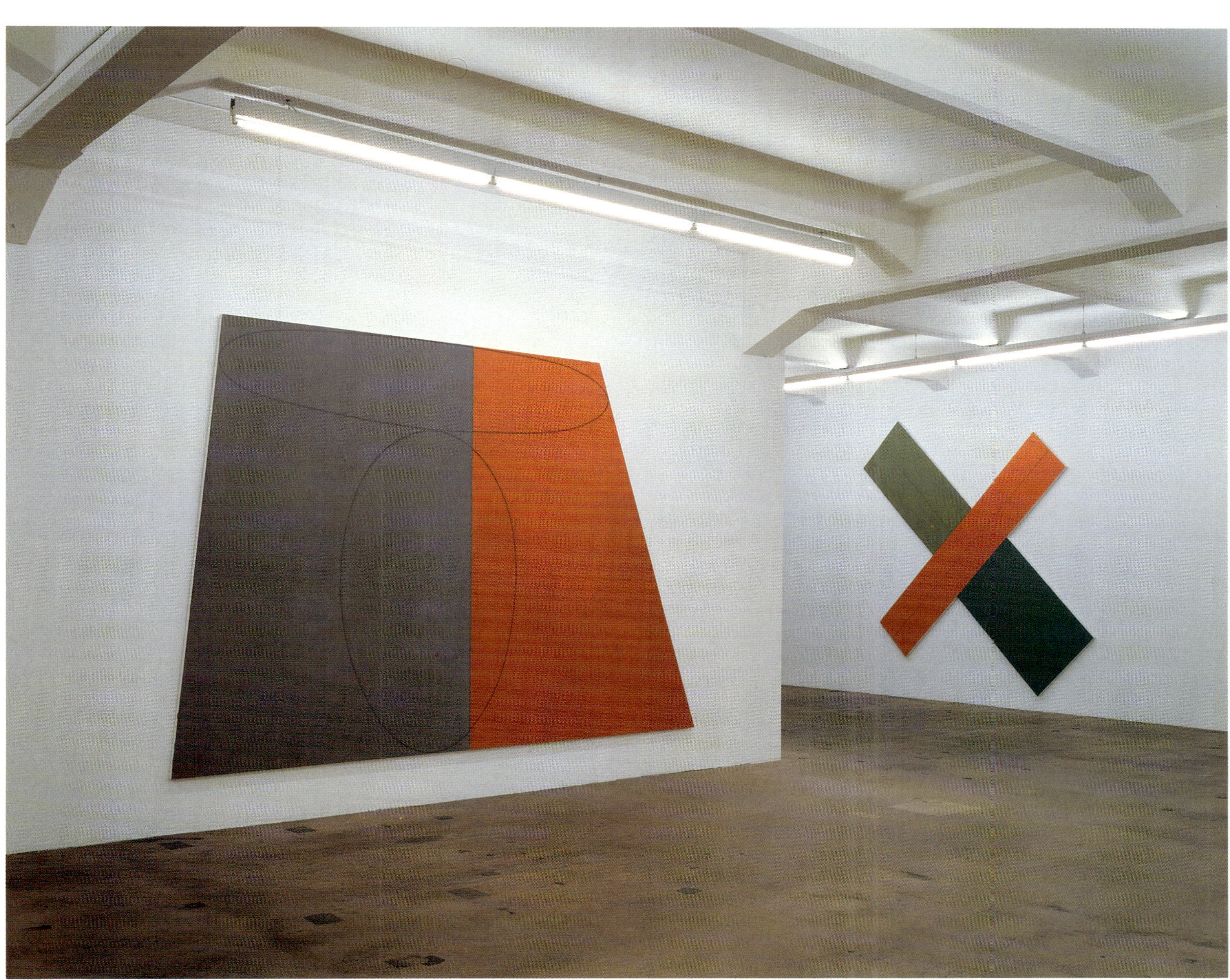

Plane/Figure Series C (Double Panel) Study 2, 1993
acrylic and black pencil on canvas, 56 x 84¼"

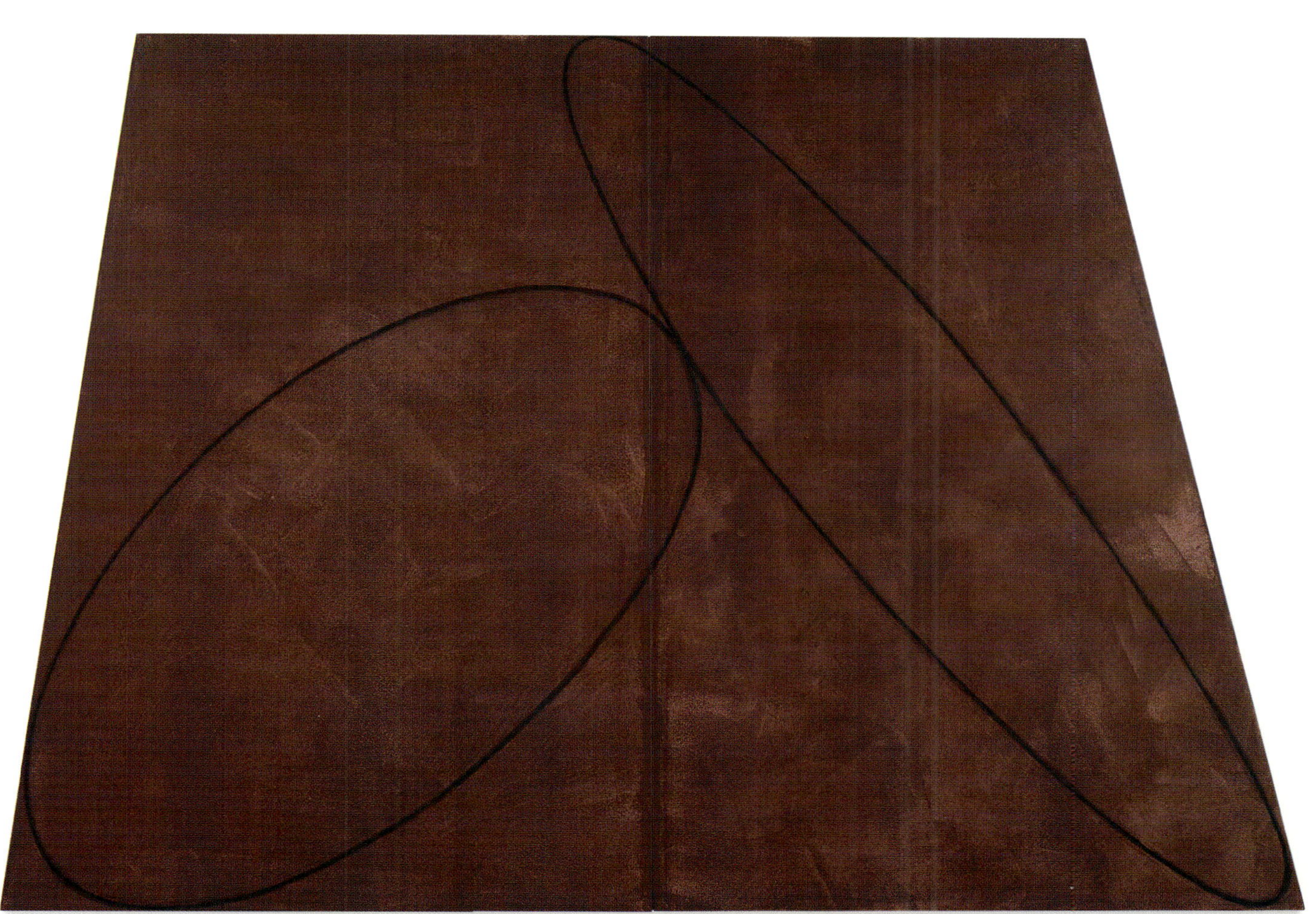

Plane/Figure Series C (Double Panel), 1993
acrylic and black pencil on canvas, 112 x 168"

Plane/Figure Series D (Double Panel), 1993
acrylic and black pencil on canvas, 112 x 168"

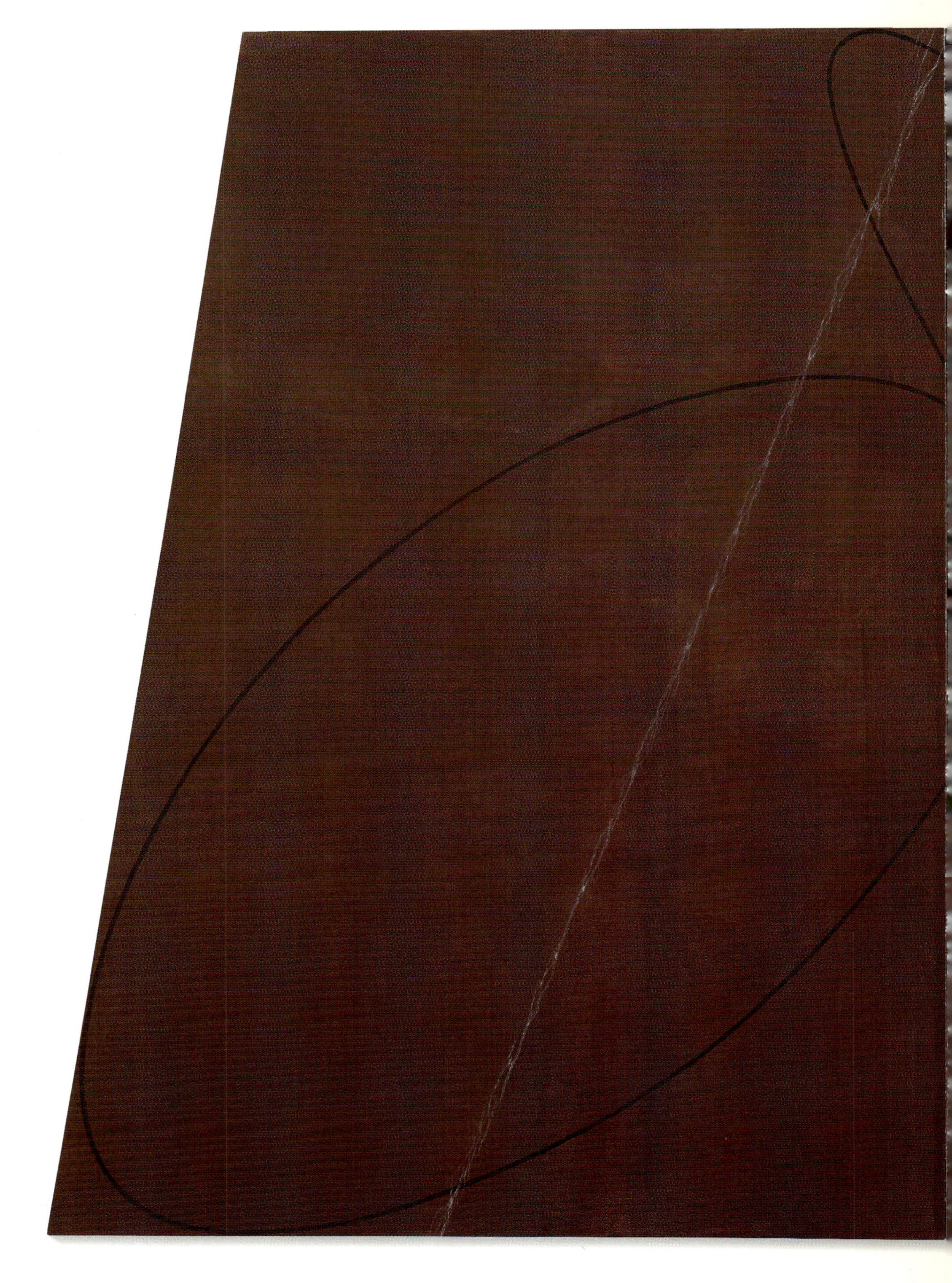

Plane/Figure Series E (Double Panel), 1993
acrylic and black pencil on canvas, 84 x 126"

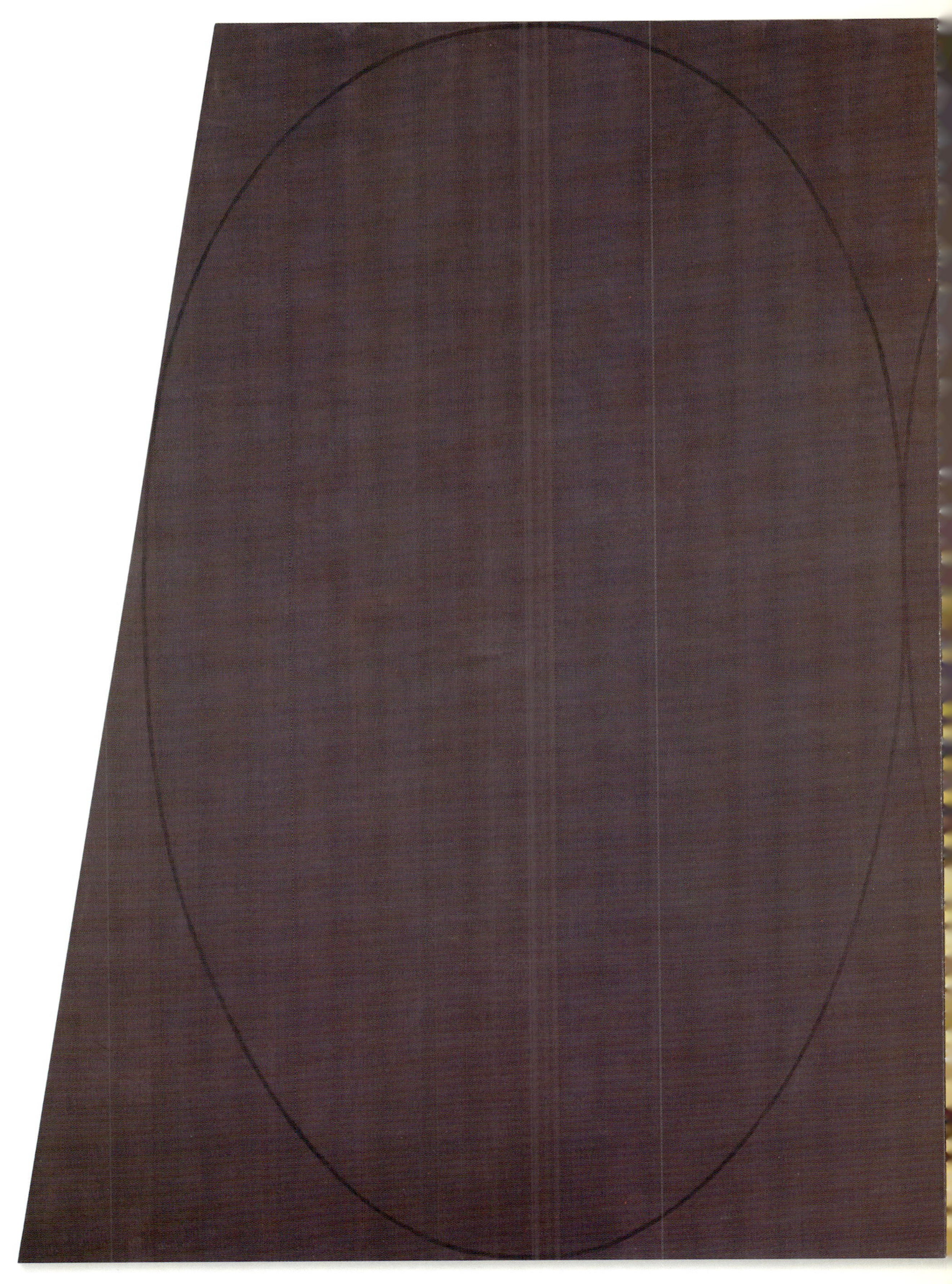

Plane/Figure Series E (Double Panel), 1993
acrylic and black pencil on canvas, 84 x 126"

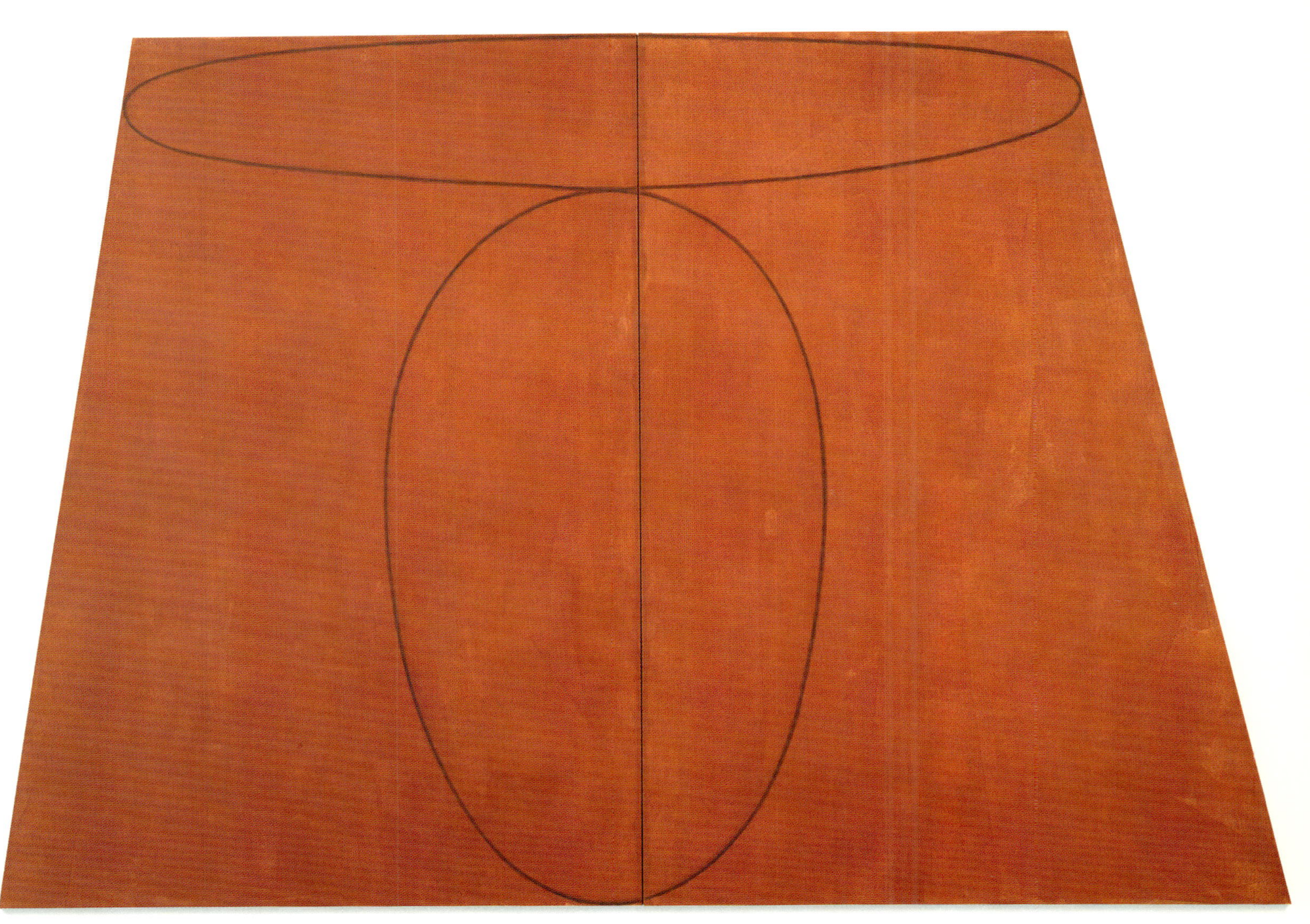

Plane/Figure Series F (Double Panel) First Version, 1993
acrylic and black pencil on canvas, 72 x 108"

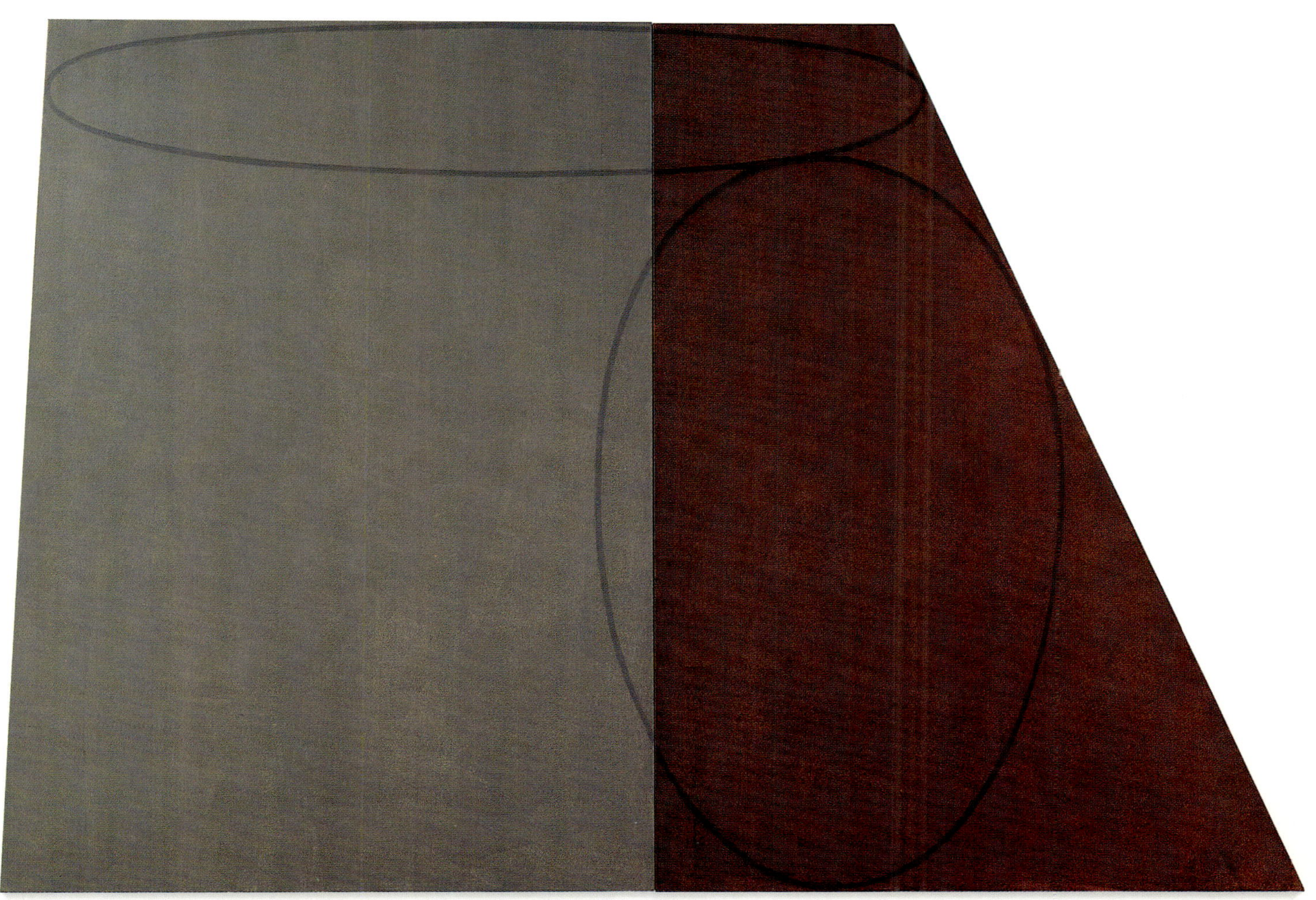

Plane/Figure Series F (Double Panel), 1993
acrylic and black pencil on canvas, 108 x 162"

Plane/Figure Series G (Double Panel), 1994
acrylic and black pencil on canvas, 84 x 98"

34

Plane/Figure Series G (Double Panel), 1994
acrylic and black pencil on canvas, 84 x 98"

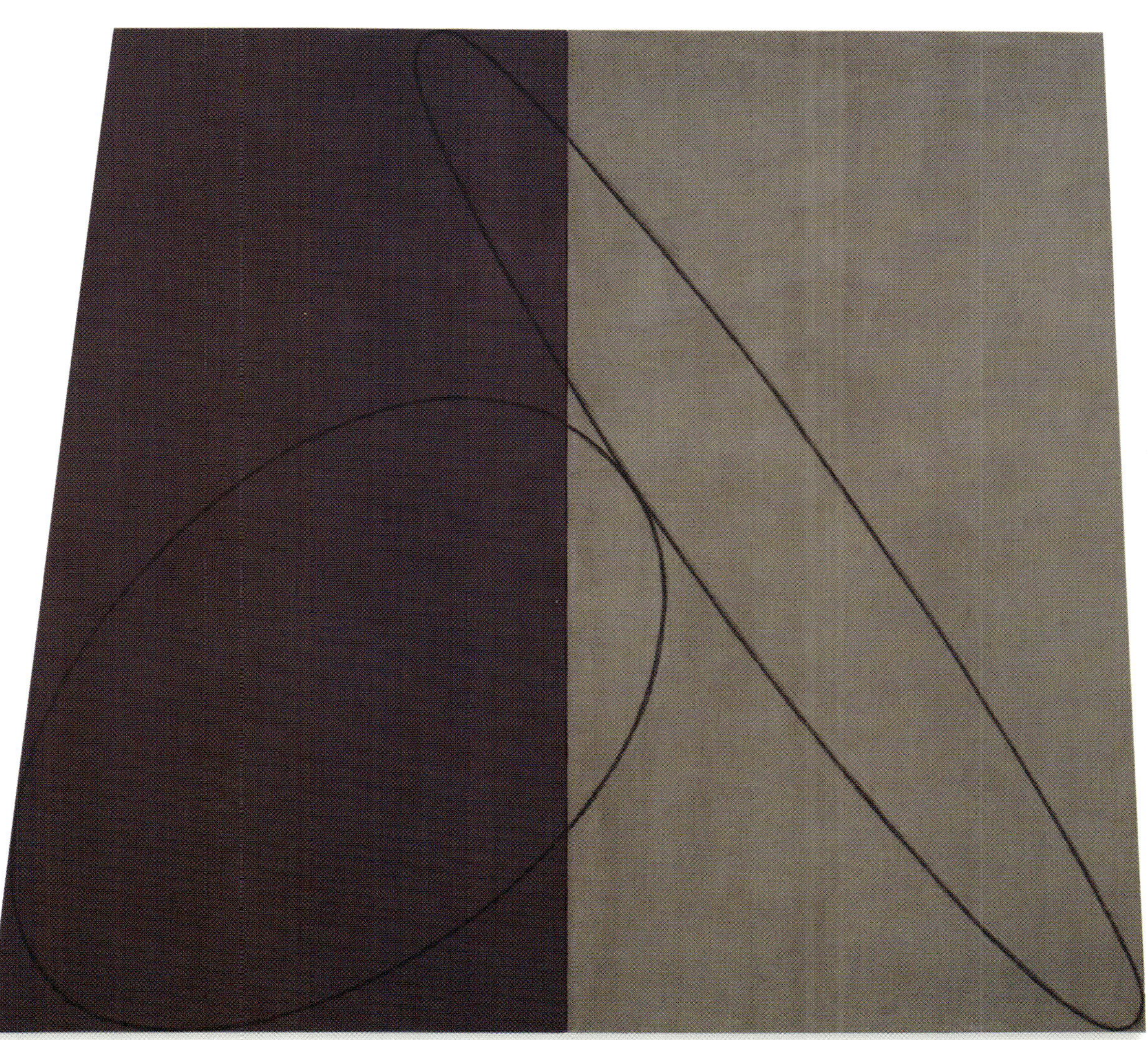

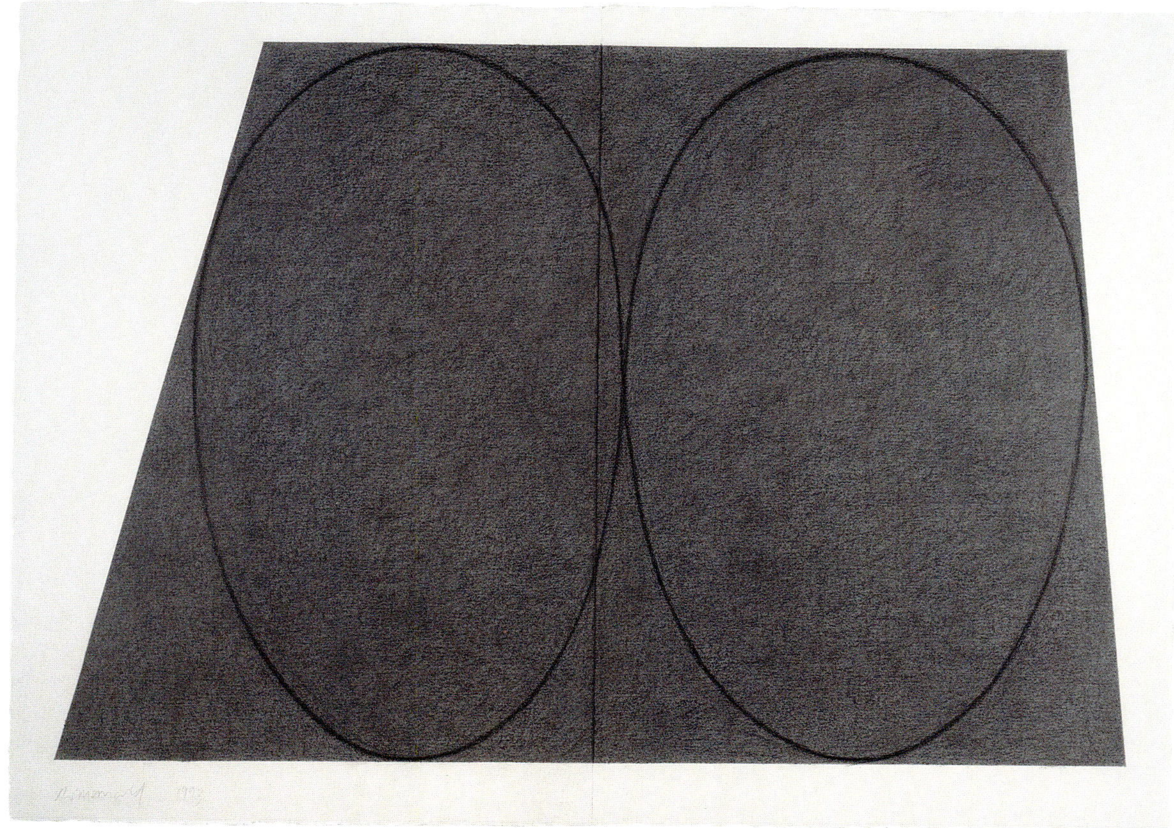

Plane/Figure, 1993
graphite on paper, 41$\frac{1}{2}$ x 58$\frac{1}{2}$"

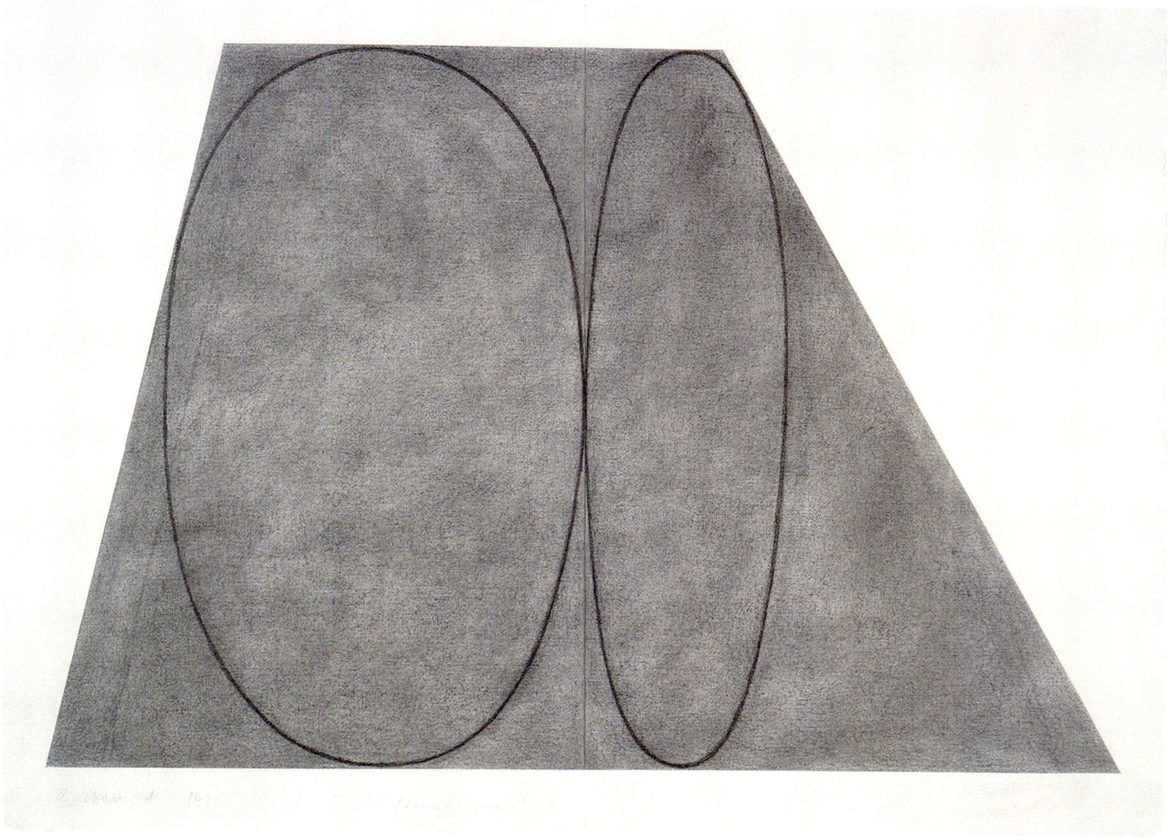

Plane/Figure, 1992
graphite on paper, 41½ x 58½"

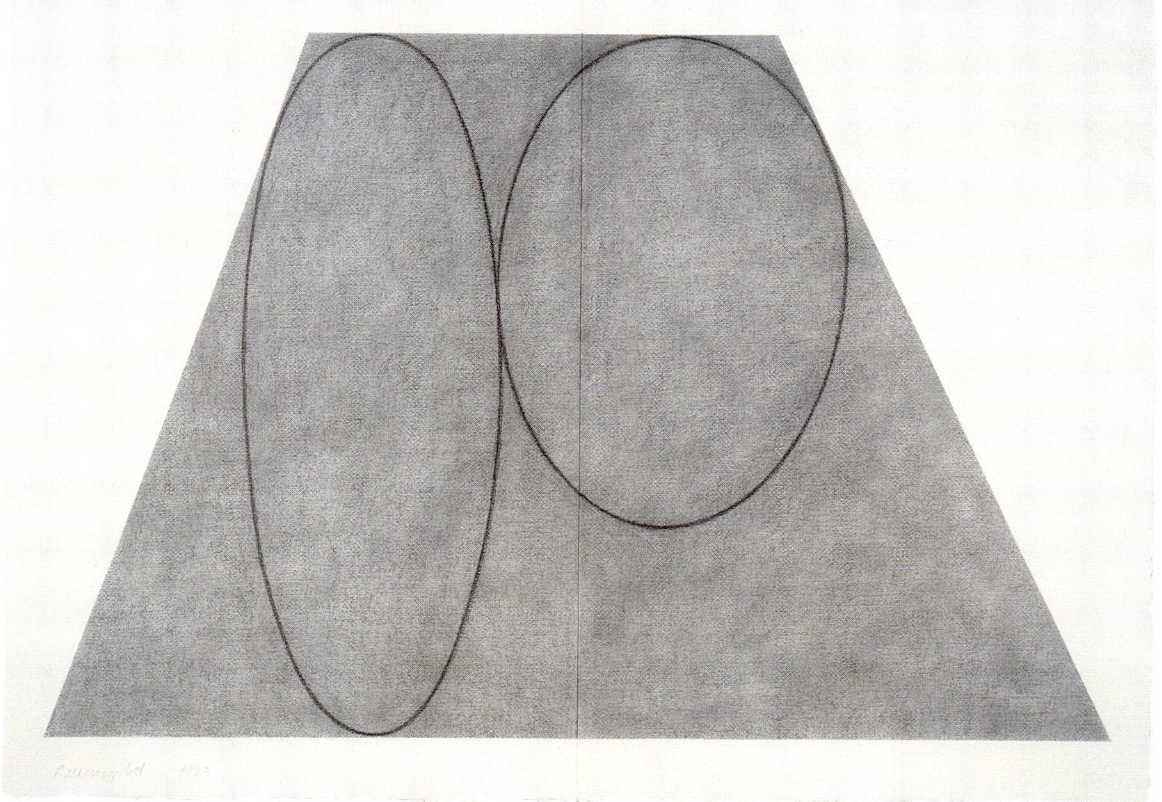

Plane/Figure, 1993
graphite on paper, 41$\frac{1}{2}$ x 58$\frac{1}{2}$"

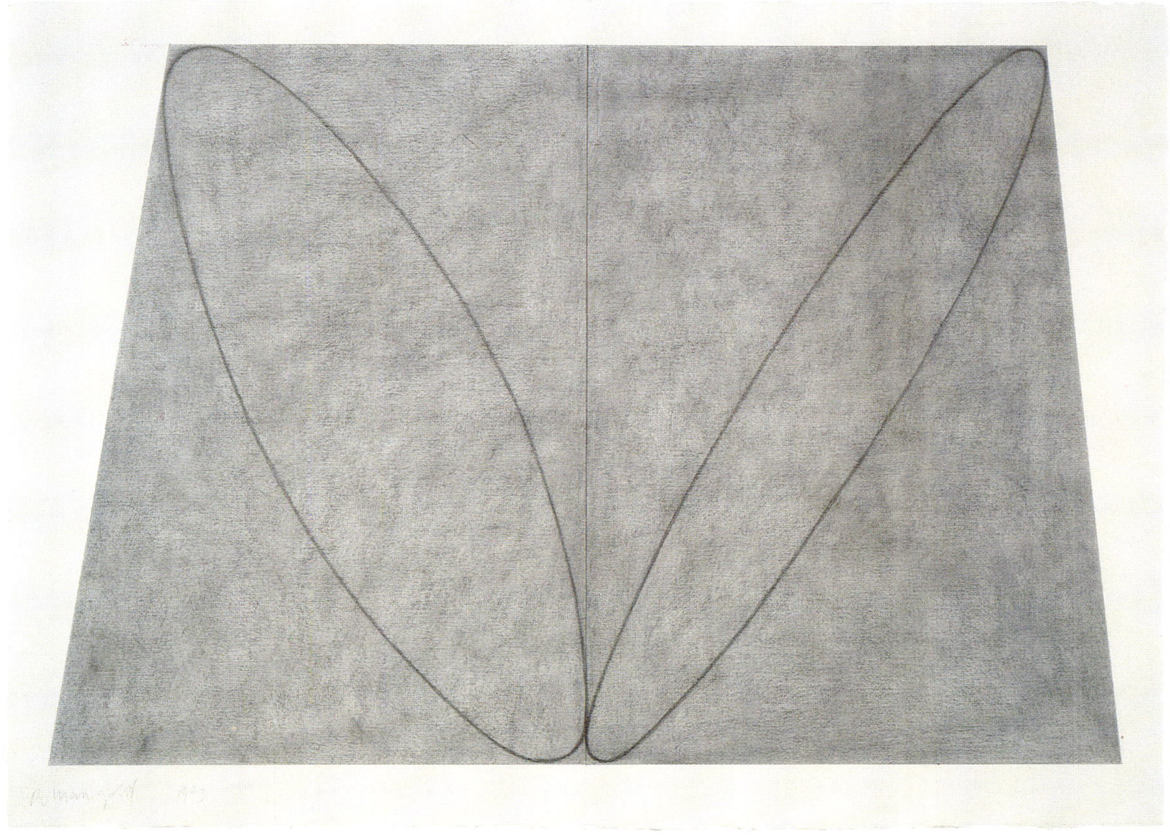

Plane/Figure, 1993
graphite on paper, 41½ x 58½″

LIST OF REPRODUCTIONS

Page 11: **Plane/Figure Series A (Double Panel) Study**, 1993, acrylic and black pencil on canvas, 56¼ x 84¼"

Page 13: **Plane/Figure Series B (Double Panel) Study**, 1993, acrylic and black pencil on canvas, 56¼ x 84½"

Page 15: **Plane/Figure Series B (Double Panel)**, 1993, acrylic and black pencil on canvas, 112 x 168"
Installation at Hallen für neue Kunst, Schaffhausen, Switzerland, 1993.

X within X, 1981, acrylic and black pencil on canvas, 152 x 128"
Installation at Hallen für neue Kunst, Schaffhausen, Switzerland, 1993. Collection Stedelijk Museum, Amsterdam.

Page 17: **Plane/Figure Series C (Double Panel) Study 2**, 1993, acrylic and black pencil on canvas, 56 x 84¼"

Page 19: **Plane/Figure Series C (Double Panel)**, 1993, acrylic and black pencil on canvas, 112 x 168"

Page 23: **Plane/Figure Series D (Double Panel)**, 1993, acrylic and black pencil on canvas, 112 x 168"

Page 27: **Plane/Figure Series E (Double Panel)**, 1993, acrylic and black pencil on canvas, 84 x 126"

Page 29: **Plane/Figure Series F (Double Panel) First Version**, 1993, acrylic and black pencil on canvas, 72 x 108"

Page 31: **Plane/Figure Series F (Double Panel)**, 1993, acrylic and black pencil on canvas, 108 x 162"
Collection Bonnefantenmuseum, Maastricht, Netherlands

Page 35: **Plane/Figure Series G (Double Panel)**, 1994, acrylic and black pencil on canvas, 84 x 98"

Page 36: **Plane/Figure**, 1993, graphite on paper, 41½ x 58½"

Page 37: **Plane/Figure**, 1992, graphite on paper, 41½ x 58½"

Page 38: **Plane/Figure**, 1993, graphite on paper, 41½ x 58½"

Page 39: **Plane/Figure**, 1993, graphite on paper, 41½ x 58½"

Photography of art work by Ellen Page Wilson
Cover: detail of **Plane/Figure Series D (Double Panel)**, 1993
acrylic and black pencil on canvas, 112 x 168"

Catalogue designed and produced by
Tomoko Makiura and Paul Pollard for PaceWildenstein.

Library of Congress Catalog Card Number: 94-65714
ISBN: 1-878283-41-3